Global Anti-Corruption & Anti-Bribery Leadership

Practical FCPA and U.K. Bribery Act Compliance Concepts for the Corporate Board Member, C-Suite Executive and General Counsel

Global Anti-Corruption &

Anti-Bribery Leadership

By Thomas Fox and Jon Rydberg

Edited by Nick Briere

Copyright © 2013 Thomas Fox and Jon Rydberg

ISBN-13: 978-1494763251

TABLE OF CONTENTS

Page Number

Who Should Read This Book

If you "believe" your organization is compliant because: (1) you provided training; (2) you have an "honest" culture; or (3) because a Federal investigator hasn't told you otherwise, you may be putting the corporate enterprise at increased risk. There is a big difference between being "compliant" and having a "Compliance Program."

This book provides practical lessons pertaining to the FCPA, U.K. Bribery Act and broader Anti-Corruption / Anti-Bribery standards for Board Members, Chief Executive Officers, General Counsel and other corporate executives who seek to lower their enterprise risk profile by learning simple strategies from tested compliance veterans.

About the Authors

Thomas Fox, Principal of TomFoxLaw and Author

Mr. Fox has practiced law in Houston for 30 years. He is now assisting companies with FCPA compliance, risk management, and international transactions. He was most recently the General Counsel at Drilling Controls, Inc., a worldwide oilfield manufacturing and service company. He was previously Division Counsel with Halliburton Energy Services, Inc.

Mr. Fox is the founder and editor of the award winning *FCPA Compliance and Ethics Blog* (http://tfoxlaw.wordpress.com/). He has published three books on anti-bribery and anti-corruption issues: *Lessons Learned on Compliance and Ethics, Best Practices Under the FCPA and Bribery Act,* and *GSK in China: A Game Changer in Compliance.* He is a regular speaker, the author of a wide range of articles on these issues, and an avid maven on the use of social media for compliance. He podcasts at *The FCPA Compliance and Ethics Report* and can be reached at tfox@tfoxlaw.com.

Jon Rydberg, CEO of Orchid Advisors and Author

Mr. Rydberg has served as a global Big 4 audit, compliance, and business consulting executive for approximately 20 years. He was most recently the Chief Compliance Officer and VP, Internal Audit at Smith & Wesson and was previously employed by such leaders as Ernst & Young, Protiviti, and United Technologies, a worldwide Fortune 50 conglomerate. He served public Board members, CEOs and CFOs on high profile matters pertaining to corporate fraud and SEC financial reporting scandals, Federal FCPA investigations, Sarbanes-Oxley material weakness remediation and the optimization of internal audit programs for billion dollar entities.

Mr. Rydberg was responsible for implementing a full-scale compliance and anti-corruption/anti-bribery program in the wake of an industry-wide DOJ/SEC-led FCPA sting. He is also author of *The Four Pillars of Firearm Compliance,* a text focused on transforming ATF compliance in the Firearms Industry and has featured in such media sites as the Wall Street Journal and CNBC.

Mr. Rydberg also served in the role of global Aerospace & Defense industry practice leader and held additional positions with the Department of Homeland Security (DHS) Manufacturing Industry Sector Board and as an Executive Committee Member of the DHS Manufacturing Supply Chain Team, APICS, the IIA and Mensa. He holds a Secret Clearance and is a Certified Management Accountant (CMA), Certified Production and Inventory Management (CPIM),

Project Management Professional (PMP), and a Certified Internal Auditor (CIA). And, he holds three U.S. Patents and is a BSME, MBA and MACC (partial).

Mr. Rydberg is now transforming the Compliance Ecosystem™ as CEO of Orchid Advisors, a strategic management consultancy focused on transforming the worlds of audit and compliance. The firm provides experts in ATF compliance, State firearms compliance, anti-corruption/bribery, ITAR, import, export, and Sarbanes-Oxley. Its early entry market is the Firearms Industry, where Orchid counts among its customers the top manufacturers in the world. Orchid clients hire the firm to reinvent business processes, implement technology and big data solutions to support that change, and transform their compliance culture. Orchid Advisors brings the depth and breadth of Big Four consulting with the innovation, thought leadership, and economies of a boutique analyst firm. More information about the firm's four service lines of Compliance Consulting, Compliance Technology, Business Consulting, and Internal Audit may be found at www.orchidadvisors.com.

> **"Put simply, the prospect of significant prison sentences for individuals should make clear to every corporate executive, every board member, and every employee that we seek to hold you personally accountable for FCPA violations."**

Lanny Breuer, Assistant Attorney General, Criminal Division, U.S. Department of Justice, February 2010

In 2010, Mr. Breuer made the full-bodied statement above. Using language that lacked the slightest hint of normal "government-speak," he made it very clear that any individual caught violating the Foreign Corrupt Practices Act (FCPA) would be held accountable for his or her actions and that the U.S. Department of Justice's (DOJ) enforcement of the FCPA would include the full force of the U.S. government.

One would think that "the prospect of significant prison sentences" would go a long way toward establishing an effective deterrent. So why then are U.S. organizations continually levied billions of dollars in fines for violations of the Foreign Corrupt Practices Act?

If the mantra "Simply put, don't bribe" holds true, then maintaining compliance should be easy, right? Not necessarily. The Federal Government has established what it believes is a reasonable standard for preventing and detecting non-compliant behavior pertinent to any Federal regulation. Organizations that conduct business in the U.S. or abroad must protect their stakeholders and shareholders by meeting or exceeding the standards set forth in the Federal Sentencing Guidelines §8b2.1, "[An] Effective Compliance and Ethics Program."

Federal investigations are long. They are costly. They are painful and impact more than just your legal department. Imagine losing the ability to ship to key markets for an extended period of time. Would you like an independent monitor watching every employee transaction across your enterprise? Our guess is probably not.

Although global anti-corruption/anti-bribery standards are quickly developing and taking hold around the world, the standards and cultural norms for operating a global business still vary widely. Until those standards become uniform, and until human nature ceases to be human nature, compliance with the FCPA and similar anti-corruption/anti-bribery regulations shouldn't rest exclusively on training and a "faith in compliance."

Additionally, one of our chief reasons for writing this book was to reinforce the belief that compliance – both in general and as it pertains to the anti-corruption/anti-compliance – should be viewed, like quality and safety, as an equal business metric. Although compliance should _not_ be designed to impede efficient business operations, it should be part of the decision-making process. In fact, best-in-class compliance programs are enablers of planned and measured risk-taking.

Finally, this book is in no way meant to serve as a legal reference, nor as a formal interpretation of law. For any questions pertaining to the interpretation of global anti-corruption and anti-bribery standards, the reader should seek out the advice of a qualified legal professional.

Before you begin, take out a pen and piece of paper. Document your answers to these questions and we will compare your level of understanding at the end of our book.

- How does your organization limit the risk of non-compliance? Can you list the controls?
- Do you know what the prevailing standard and U.S. Government expectations are for a compliance program?
- Can you point to (or touch) your compliance program? What about your ethics program?
- How do you mitigate the risk of bribery?
- How do you mitigate inappropriate disbursements?
- When was your last independent anti-corruption/anti-bribery program audit?

The high volume of fines levied by the U.S. government resulting from investigations into violations of the Foreign Corrupt Practices Act demonstrates the extent and maturity of existing U.S. anti-corruption/anti-bribery programs, as well as the extent of pain felt across the corporate landscape.

When asked, "What element of FCPA compliance do organizations lack most?" we often respond with "Confusion between the concepts of Compliance and a Compliance Program." Some organizations simply don't know the difference.

- Do companies really understand the requirements of a robust anti-corruption/anti-compliance compliance program?
- Do they understand where the company stands in terms of compliance with prevailing laws such as the FCPA and U.K. Bribery Act?
- Do they understand related laws in other local countries in which they conduct business transactions?
- Do they understand the risks of being non-compliant?
- Is the company engaging in risky behavior in its dealings overseas, and if so, are they aware of it?
- Do companies have real-time visibility into their transactions with monitoring dashboards?

We once had a client that asked for an evaluation of their Ethics Program. After a short review, it was concluded that a *Program* did not exist. The Vice President of Human Resources was angered by the conclusion. "How can you say that? We are run like a family – our employees are trustworthy and we are definitely ethical and compliant." We asked again, as a Federal investigator would, "Can you please provide us with evidence of your Ethics *Program*?" The client could point to nothing other than training and a family-oriented culture.

Obviously anti-corruption/anti-bribery training is important – but the DOJ's expectation includes the existence of *Program* elements as listed in §8b2.1. That means something tangible, promoted, audited, measured, and improved.

Granted, it is difficult to control the behavior of every employee, contractor, or sales agent in a large, international organization; but there must be a higher level of awareness and institutional priority around building and maintaining an effective program. This simply is not optional.

More appropriately stated, compliance, like quality, safety, and ethics, must be *embedded* into the fabric of the business. These elements all should have the underlying foundation in the organization's Mission, Vision, Values, and Code of Conduct, and end with a *continuous* and *transparent* evaluation of itself.

The DOJ and the Securities and Exchange Commission (SEC) assess an average of 50+ U.S. FCPA violation cases each year. And while that may not seem like a large number considering how many U.S. firms operate internationally, it's a huge caseload for the Federal regulators because of the time and resources necessary to mount an FCPA investigation.

The consequences of an FCPA violation are serious. An individual found in violation of FCPA can be sentenced to five years in prison and fined up to $250,000 per instance of violation; companies can be fined up to $2 million per instance. An FCPA investigation could involve dozens or hundreds of instances. Even if there is no prison sentence, the fines alone can add up quickly. But perhaps most impactful is: (1) Public announcement of the investigation; (2) Derivative lawsuits; (3) Inability to sell into key markets; (4) loss of long-term relationships; and (5) The threat of an independent monitor. Is it really worth it?

While the fines can be very expensive and the threat of prison time is enough make anyone nervous, the real cost is in the personal and professional years lost while under investigation. The DOJ and SEC have been known to be slow and deliberative in their investigative process. Consequently, a company under investigation can expect to expend incredible amounts of time and resources to fulfill investigator needs.

Part of what makes these investigations so incredibly detailed and time-consuming is that the process of interpreting violations can be very subjective. For instance, the U.S. law speaks to the "intent to bribe." How does the Government determine that a company and its employees had the *intent* to bribe? Investigators end up pouring over hundreds of thousands—if not millions—of emails, trying to interpret possible out-of-context words an employee used in conversation years ago. Was that person joking or serious? Did this conversation represent the intent to bribe? These are hard questions to answer.

There is a growing focus on the part of worldwide governments and businesses alike on the subject of anti-bribery and anti-corruption. The two most prevalent legislative efforts toward progressing this goal are the U.S. Foreign Corrupt Practices Act and the U.K. Bribery Act.

The Foreign Corrupt Practices Act of 1977 was enacted by the U.S. Congress and signed into law by President Jimmy Carter with the goal of stopping what had become a pattern of bribery, particularly the bribing of foreign officials by U.S. companies and individuals. The impetus for creating the FCPA arose out of extensive investigations in the 1970s by the SEC, which found more than 400 U.S. companies admitting to illegal (or, at minimum, "questionable") payments to foreign officials. These payments were made to induce favorable business outcomes and amounted to more than $300 million. At the time, the act of bribery was not technically illegal; however, the act hiding such behavior from a company's shareholders was, and brought the scandal to both the SEC's and public's attention. This contributed heavily to an atmosphere of anti-corruption and lead to the adoption of the Foreign Corrupt Practices Act. Regardless of the laws – then or now – we all know that bribery and corruption are both irrevocably unethical and that leaders should seek to exclude them from their organizations.

Understanding the Foreign Corrupt Practices Act

The Foreign Corrupt Practices Act is about bribery, plain and simple. There are two prominent themes of the FCPA. The first, the **anti-bribery provisions**, makes it illegal to bribe any foreign official. The second, the **books and records provision,** mandates that companies keep accurate records pertaining to transactions involving foreign business activity, notwithstanding existing SEC rules relating to the accuracy of all financial recordkeeping.

Anti-Bribery Provisions

Simply stated, the FCPA makes it illegal for a U.S. company or individual to bribe a foreign official. The definition of foreign official is broad and can include government officials and their family members, administrators at a government-owned or managed institution, and quasi-government agencies that are owned both privately and by local governments. Also falling under the jurisdiction of the FCPA are employees of international organizations, like the United Nations.

Under the Act, a bribe is the offer of anything of value – cash, merchandise, property, services, etc. The real focus is on the *intent* to bribe or influence, not on the amount or value of the bribe (or even whether or not the bribe ultimately took place or if any benefit was received). It is also illegal to have any knowledge of a bribe, to supervise a bribe, or to fail to report a bribe. In short, pretty much anything associated with bribery of a foreign official is illegal under the FCPA. The only exceptions are in some pretty extreme hostage situations—so extreme that they really aren't germane to this book.

Books and Records Provisions

The FCPA also requires companies whose securities are listed in the United States to make and keep books and records that accurately and fairly reflect the transactions of the corporation and maintain an adequate system of internal accounting controls. In essence, if a company is conducting business with foreign entities, it must be able to substantiate and produce records for any overseas transactions. These transactions range from travel and entertainment, to free product, to international offsets, to agent sales commissions, and to everything in between.

These accounting provisions were designed to operate in tandem with the anti-bribery provisions of the FCPA and the two are often evaluated together in the course of a government-led investigation. You might read the above paragraphs and believe the FCPA is not applicable to you and/or your organization. "We don't conduct business with foreign governments and therefore this is not of concern." On the contrary. Take the following, for example:

- A bribe or any intent to influence a transaction whose end user, buyer, or decision maker is unrelated to a foreign government may still be subject to the same level of legal risk.
- The government may view your domestic distributors, who sell internationally, as legal extensions of your organization although they are technically not. Whom you do business with and the expectations that you establish with those parties are subject to such concern.

The U.K. Bribery Act

Globally, the standards for anti-bribery have broadened far beyond the FCPA and should be viewed in the general context of anti-corruption, anti-bribery, or even as a core tenant in corporate ethics. The U.K. Bribery Act is the most prominent expansion from the U.S. rules, in which the historical view about "bribery with foreign officials" is greatly expanded upon to include not only organizations and governments but individuals and commercial transactions as well.

If one wanted evidence that the world is evolving toward fighting bribery and corruption, the U.K. Bribery Act would be a great indicator of this trend. In 2010, the British Parliament enacted the Bribery Act 2010 (widely known as the U.K. Bribery Act). The legislation was initiated on recommendations from the British Serious Fraud Office (SFO) and, in many ways, is far more comprehensive and far-reaching than the FCPA. Businesses that base their internal anti-corruption and anti-bribery compliance programs on the U.K. Bribery Act may in fact be using a more comprehensive standard.

This is because the U.K. Bribery Act goes much further than the FCPA. Unlike the FCPA, the U.K. Bribery Act prohibits any type of bribery whatsoever. It doesn't matter if it's bribery of a foreign citizen, a domestic citizen, a foreign government official or a domestic one. It doesn't matter if it's a corporation or a neighbor; bribery of any kind is prohibited.

The Growing Anti-Bribery/Anti-Corruption Push Around The Globe

The world is truly becoming a global marketplace. With multi-million international business deals affecting the lives and safety of the public, there is an ever-increasing need for common standards and practices. There is a push to establish such common standards in many industries – a good example is the International Financial Reporting Standard (IFRS), which has been advocated to establish standardization in financial reporting between U.S. and international companies. It's evidence that the world is connecting.

This big-picture and global trend toward interconnectivity is affecting the way corruption and bribery are perceived and treated in countries all around the world.

Anti-corruption and anti-bribery regulations are emerging in countries globally – even in countries where it had never really been a prominent concern. In some cases, this conflicts with the cultural norms of nations that rely on offering something of value in exchange for a desired outcome. In some places, that is just the way things are done; it's the way of business, a cultural heritage. However, a key goal of this globalization of ethics is for every country in the world to make the bribery of its own government officials illegal.

If there was ever any doubt as to this singular need, consider the recent investigations in China over Western companies led by GlaxoSmithKline (GSK). The Chinese government announced they would no longer tolerate Western companies engaging in bribery and corruption of their government officials. The key point from the GSK case is that the Chinese enforced their own domestic anti-bribery laws.

So now companies can face prosecution under the FCPA, U.K. Bribery Act, or a country's domestic law for engaging in bribery and corruption.

The business environment is changing and laws surrounding bribery, corruption, and ethics are growing in complexity, necessitating a comprehensive program to ensure compliance with the FCPA (at minimum).

In order to design an effective anti-corruption/anti-bribery program, it is critical that you understand and define the nature of your business. Consider, for example, such issues as who are you selling to, how you sell to them, and what is your sales and distribution model?

As rudimentary as it might seem, the answers can have a significant impact on the complexity of your final program. Let's look at these issues now.

Who are you selling to?

A company that sells directly to commercial third parties or consumers, never interacting with any government officials in any foreign country, has less FCPA risk than a company that contracts with or sells to a foreign official, engaged in third party negotiations or uses offsets as contractual obligations. Sounds basic, but "Who are you selling to?" is a key first question to ask yourself.

The question should consider the following non-exhaustive list of buyer types:

- Domestic commercial
- Domestic government
- International commercial
- International government
- Quasi-international government (part private, part government)
- U.S. Government-sponsored sales to international governments
- U.S. or international government agents for personal use
- Government or commercially-run buying groups

Each of these scenarios brings with it its own set of risks and design considerations for your program. Do you know, for example, how to handle transactions with quasi-government bodies? What are the rules? And if you don't know, how do you think your sales personnel and accounts payable team will know?

How do you sell?

The nature of your sales process can vary widely. Much of that is driven by the industry in which you operate and the nature of the "offering." In other words, are you selling products, services, or both? These offerings can be sold in a number of ways, but consider the varied risk profile in the following models, ranked from lowest to highest risk.

- Retail Point of Sale (POS) – **Potentially lowest risk**
- Commercial purchase order/invoice (with or without a contract)
- Fixed price or time and material arrangements
- Catalogue pricing
- Discounted pricing
- Volume-based pricing with free, good incentives
- Negotiated pricing
- Pricing with built-in promises of return, such as International Offset programs or accompanied free goods
- Bartering in the sales process
- Inclusion of suppliers or other parties in the sales process
- Use of warranty centers
- License of your product through international manufacturers
- Use of other business partners or joint venture partners
- Use of third party lobbyists or distant contract "sales consultants" – **Potentially highest risk**

This list could go on to include a few more, but the point is clear. A retail point of sales transaction is less likely to include opportunities for bribery. A negotiated contract with discounted pricing, in which you pay a third party to prepare a proposal and interact with a foreign government on your behalf, would offer relatively higher risk.

What is your sales and distribution model?

Do you sell directly to end-users? Or do you sell through wholesalers, distributors, and retailers? Do you use an internal sales force or third party commissioned sales agents? Commissioned sales agents will definitely add complexity to the mix and could be highly scrutinized by regulators.

What commission is "appropriate" depends on many factors, including the culture of the country in which you are doing business and the nature the industry. The first question that a regulator might ask is about sales commission and the determination of how "excessive" it is (or isn't). Of course, that is a question with frequently subjective answer. In some industries, the "business norm" for commissions can be in the "1% to 5%" range, while in others the norm may be in the "25% to 30%" range. The respective government might consider the latter to be "a lot of money," and consequently will see incentive to consummate a deal. Consider your commission structure and the appropriateness of amount in the context of your operating environment. More importantly, determine if the commission can be tied to some tangible work product or a process/service that added value to the transaction.

If you're a manufacturer, you might sell to a distributor at a reduced cost. This distributor will then likely sell the product with a profitable markup. Depending on market conditions, it would be common to offer such distributors additional discounts, volume purchases, or other kinds of business norms when operating in a foreign country. "What does the distributor do with that extra money?" a regulatory might ask. "Is it simply profit? Or is it being used to influence a foreign official?" Your distribution contracts need to spell out the acceptable uses of any discounts or promotional funds to avoid any potential FCPA violations.

Suffice it to say that different industries will have different risk profiles. Take the construction industry for example. With huge infrastructure projects all over the world, construction firms can have a higher-than-average FCPA risk profile.

Why? First, most of the contracts are administered by or through the foreign government, quasi-government entities, and government officials. Second, the method by which the contracts are paid can be complicated—many are based on adherence to a set schedule, offering monetary incentives for on-time completion. It can be difficult to truly value the services rendered.

You need to define the industry in which you operate (and its level of risk), the part of the world in which you are operating (this will define the prevalence of corruption), to whom you are selling products or services, how many steps there are in the distribution model, and who are the parties are and how they are connected to you.

A critical consideration to understanding your business risk is identifying where on the globe you operate. Transparency International (www.transparency.org/) is an organization that studies and monitors the relative level of corruption around the world on a country-by-country basis. The organization generates a Corruption Performance Index (CPI, www.transparency.org/research/cpi/overview) which ranks countries on their corruption levels, ranging from Singapore as a low risk/low corruption environment, to Afghanistan and Iraq which represent high risk/high corruption environments. It's critical to measure environmental considerations—that is to say, the political and economic stability of the geographic environment in which you're doing business. Is corruption a part of their culture? As you can imagine, some foreign governments are corrupt themselves and might require bribes in order to do business in or with their country.

We know you've provided "FCPA Training" to your organization, but is your program designed with internal controls that are individually applicable to the scenarios noted above?

Remember, you're responsible for running your business in a way that is compliant with the anti-corruption and anti-bribery standards. It doesn't matter what everyone else is doing or what is culturally acceptable. The excuses "I didn't know it was wrong" or "We trained our people" won't suffice.

The underlying principles of every anti-corruption/anti-bribery program should be the same. That is, the regulations and requirements with which you're required to comply remain predominantly the same. The risk profile, extent of controls, and methods/tools deployed are what vary.

However, implementing a program that meets the necessary standards in a practical way can be a complicated, multi-year endeavor, requiring continued adjustment and maintenance. Sure, there's a basic structure; but there is no ready-to-go, "one size fits all" anti-corruption/anti-bribery program.

<u>Establishing A Framework</u>

The Federal Government has clear expectations for what defines an "effective compliance and ethics program." As noted earlier, those expectations are clearly outlined in Chapter 8, Part B 2.1 of the Federal Sentencing Guidelines (www.ussc.gov/Guidelines/) and include the following as paraphrased:

- Leadership and Tone from The Top
- A Commitment to Compliance – Beyond the Tone
- Measurement: Set at Zero Tolerance; There is No Materiality Standard for Corruption and Bribery
- Standards and Procedures
- Education and Training
- Efforts to Exclude Prohibited Personnel with Due Diligence
- Validation and Oversight

Let's review each of these in turn.

<u>Leadership and Tone at the Top</u>

Both the U.S. Federal Sentencing Guidelines and the Organization for Economic Co-operation and Development's (OECD) *Good Practice Guidance on Internal Controls, Ethics, and Compliance* consider a best practice program to start with an unbreakable "Tone at the Top."

The FSG reads: "High-level personnel and substantial authority personnel of the organization shall be knowledgeable about the content and operation of the compliance and ethics program ... and shall promote an organizational culture that encourages ethical conduct and a commitment to compliance with the law."

The OECD Good Practice Guidance reads: "Strong, explicit and visible support and commitment from senior management to the company's internal controls, ethics and compliance programs or measures for preventing and detecting foreign bribery."

Everyone understands that a company leader must set the tone that the entity will not engage in corruption or bribery. However, "tone-at-the-top" encompasses more than simply saying the right things. It represents a *commitment to compliance*, far beyond the "tone."

<u>A Commitment To Compliance – Beyond the Tone</u>

Compliance can be occasionally seen as a priority that competes with the achievement of top-and-bottom-line financial goals. One of the most prioritized tasks that corporate leadership can undertake is to ensure that these two elements do not compete, but rather exist synergistically. Leadership from senior executives is required to ensure that compliance objectives are achieved despite the possible distraction from competing objectives.

Typically, demonstrating such a commitment consists of any one or more of the following actions:

- Hiring of a dedicated Chief Compliance Officer who has a direct, independent reporting relationship to either the Board of Directors or the Audit Committee of the Board of Directors;
- Creating a cross-functional business and ethics council tasked with promoting a compliance and ethics program. Ideally, this council should also provide some independent oversight of higher-risk business transactions;
- Developing a respectful, collaborative working relationship between the Board, C-Suite, Internal Audit and Legal/Compliance;
- Being part of the selection and training of senior managers to lead anti-corruption/anti-bribery work;
- Creating an independent reporting hotline ("whistleblower") and providing of methods to promote it through company posters, pamphlets, and events;
- Providing leadership on key tools, such as a code of conduct or independent auditing of one's own actions;
- Endorsing all publications related to the prevention of corruption and/or bribery;
- Leading the company in awareness and encouraging a transparent dialogue to ensure the effective dissemination of anti-bribery and anti-corruption policies and procedures to employees;

- Remaining engaged and/or involved in oversight of appropriate third party business partners;
- Demonstrating leadership through relevant external bodies—such as industry trade groups and the media—to help articulate both the company's overall compliance efforts and the industry commitment in the fight against bribery and corruption;
- Remaining involved in high profile and critical decision-making when appropriate;
- Assuring that not only is an appropriate risk assessment conducted, but that it informs the company's anti-corruption and anti-bribery compliance program;
- Demonstrating oversight of procedure violation; and,
- Providing feedback to the company's Board of Directors or equivalent, where appropriate, on levels of compliance.

A commitment to compliance can be articulated with three words: _leadership_, _ownership_, and _accountability_. Without all three concepts firmly in place, your best compliance efforts could fail.

Leadership - Demonstrated by making compliance with rules and regulations an equal metric, on par with quality, safety, and financial performance.

- Business metrics are measurable goals of an organization that establish its short or long-term direction. Although these metrics may be financially oriented, it is a best practice to run the business with a "balanced scorecard." Furthermore, at least one metric should relate to the long-term, continuous improvement of compliance, safety, and other areas that form good corporate stewardship.
- Mature organizations may use elements of Enterprise Risk Management (ERM) as a methodology for linking risk events (e.g., bribery driven by a foreign sales agent) with operational objectives (e.g., selling into a given international market).
- Compliance functions should have a voice at periodic meetings with the: Board of Directors, Audit Committee, and Executive Management team (i.e., staff meetings). Furthermore, dedicated time should be set on the agenda to ensure consistent reporting.
- Company-wide communications should balance financial, operational, and compliance matters. As with our prior recommendations, balance is critical to achieving desired outcomes. Best-in-class companies integrate company presentations with an overview of critical risk management areas, such as compliance and safety.

<u>Ownership</u> - Individual responsibilities should be established in the company's organization chart and throughout its job descriptions; otherwise, it becomes intangible and cannot be measured or managed. It is important to distinguish between those who are:

- "Responsible" for compliance: Everyone is responsible for being compliant. For example, the individuals who process sales transactions, commission payments, shipments of free goods, and shipments of finished goods have the greatest day-to-day impact on an organization's compliance. These "transaction-level" resources have as much, if not more, "responsibility" for achieving compliance.
- "Accountable" for compliance: These are the individuals that provide the resources and oversight for ensuring effective execution. They are the tone-setters and should also be held accountable for the compliance results in their functional areas. They are typically supervisors or members of management.
- "Advisors" of compliance: These are the individuals who interpret rulings and advise the business on the boundaries of compliance. They are typically members of a legal or compliance function.
- "Monitors" of compliance: These are independent personnel who are charged with the assessment of the organization's compliance with established policies and procedures. They are typically members of an audit or quality function.

<u>Accountability</u> - Without accountability, your compliance efforts could be meaningless. Directives of middle and upper-management may get ignored by those employees who know that, despite their actions, they will not be held accountable. Accountability is the glue that binds policies, procedures, and execution together.

<u>Measurement: Set at Zero Tolerance; There is No Materiality Standard for Corruption and Bribery</u>

There are several steps that a company can take to establish a zero-tolerance policy towards corruption and bribery. For instance, there could be a formal, written statement establishing policies that direct the business towards an atmosphere of integrity and compliance. In fact, there can be several forms of communication, which might be tailored to different audiences within the company. Ideally, these would be generally available on a company's intranet and internet site. Let's look at what a formal statement might include.

Cornerstones of a formal statement might include:

- A commitment to carry out business fairly, honestly, openly, and with transparency;
- A commitment to zero-tolerance towards corruption and bribery;
- The negative consequences of breaching the policy for both general employees and managers;
- The negative consequences of breaching contractual provisions relating to anti-corruption and anti-bribery prevention formally sent and/or communicated to channel partners;
- A statement of the benefits of rejecting bribery for both the company and its employees. This would include the reputation of the company with customers, the confidence of its business partners, and the incentives for employees to do business in a compliant manner;
- A clear communication that key company individuals and departments are involved in the development and implementation of the company's anti-corruption and anti-bribery prevention procedures; and,
- Reference to the company's public-facing involvement in any collective action against corruption and bribery in its business sector; or,
- A reference to the range of anti-corruption/anti-bribery prevention procedures the company has or is putting in place. This should include any protection and procedures for confidential reporting of bribery such as anonymous reporting through a helpline or hotline. This inclusion is arguably the most vital of all previously listed.

Standards and Procedures

Standards (or policies) are an organization's written rules in response to the law and/or other company expectations. *Procedures* (or work instructions) provide employees with the methods to achieve compliance with those policies.

These standards and procedures are critical towards achieving and maintaining compliance for the following reasons:

- Personnel join and leave the organization and knowledge needs to be retained;
- Lack of written standards can lead to variability in transaction quality; and,
- Employees only retain a small percentage of the information that they receive through training sessions. Written reference material is critical to increasing the likelihood that the activities of employees will remain compliant.

How does a company decide what its standards and procedures should be? Well, by asking basic questions about the business, how it works, and where it conducts business. Here are some examples:

- Will the company do business in countries with high corruption ratings, as defined by the Transparency International Corruption Perception Index?
- Will the company use an internal sales force? Or will that function be outsourced?
- If the company will use an external or outsourced sales force, will they commission based?
- Does the company offer a standard set of discounts? Or will it vary them by country?
- Does the company offer free promotional product?
- What type of individual is allowed to work for the organization and in what departments?
- What standards have been set for contractors or third party agents?

Other areas where standards need to be set include email and communications, travel and entertainment, gifts, and ethical behavior for the organization. Many of these are items are inherent to a well-written Code of Conduct and Corporate Policy set.

While there are several methods for making standards and procedures available to employees, the following key factors should be considered:

- There should be a formal process for developing, releasing, changing, and deleting policies and procedures documentation. The process should be standardized, repeatable, and, ideally, managed by an independent resource in the organization.
- All draft documentation should be reviewed by critical stakeholders of the organization. As an example, legal, compliance, and operations management should review and jointly agree upon final drafts that are then approved by higher levels of management (VPs and C-suite executives), depending on the size and structure of the organization.
- There should be a formal process for communicating new or revised policy and procedure documentation.
- There should be a formal process for controlling and distributing the policies and procedures documentation, including, but not limited to: hardcopy distribution that is maintained in a central, controlled department binder; revision-controlled handbooks that can be distributed at the employee desk level; and online and web-based repositories.

Recommended standards and procedures might, amongst others, include the following:

- A Code of Conduct and Ethics
- An Anti-Corruption /Anti-Bribery Program
- A List Of Prohibited Activities (Bribery; Corruption; Facilitation Payments; Inappropriate Political Contributions)
- Conflicts of Interest
- Gift and Gratuities
- Travel and Entertainment
- Free Goods and Promotional Activities
- Delegation of Authority and Approval Matrix
- Third Party and Employee Due Diligence Procedures
- Contract, Pricing, and Commission Standards
- Accounts Payable, Accounts Receivable, and Disbursements
- An Internal Audit Charter and Annual Internal Audit Plan
- An Audit and Investigations Policy
- A Corrective Actions Process

Education and Training

Education and training can come in many different forms. While everyone in the organization should be trained on core ethics and compliance principles, some may require deeper levels of teaching. For example, those employees involved in international sales and marketing, legal, compliance, and the accounting departments have a greater responsibility due to their roles as international transaction "control owners." Having a deeper level of knowledge becomes a great aid in stopping FCPA issues before they happen.

An organization's investment in education and training does not need to be significant in order to be effective. In fact, small investments in this area often have the greatest bang for the compliance buck. While solid business processes and system controls can limit the risk of undesired outcomes, it is the mass of employees who process transactions that have the single greatest impact on achieving compliance. Judgment often becomes a key element in doing the right thing.

How proper training is achieved is dependent upon an organization's size, technological infrastructure, and existing culture. But, regardless of those factors, there is no more effective method than a program of in-person training that provides employees with the ability to ask questions and receive direct answers.

We recommend a balanced approach to training that may include some of the following methods of delivery:

- Annual, in-person training focused on tone setting, the basic premises of the law, and areas of high risk.
- Short interval, quarterly online training used to reinforce a central message.
- On-demand training materials that can be made available through online university systems, such as Corpedia, LRN, WeComply, SkillSoft, Cogentys, SABA, Click4Compliance, and SuccessFactors, amongst others. The advantages of such materials are numerous, including long-term development of employees and the potential integration of training efforts with your suppliers and sales channel partners.
- Laminated reference materials co-located with transaction processing.
- Localized, public posting of key rules. This can be accomplished via laminated posters or desk trinkets.

Efforts to Exclude Prohibited Personnel with Due Diligence

While most compliance practitioners are certainly aware of the need to perform due diligence, they may not understand its *continued role* in third party relationships. From this perspective, they can be divided into past, present, and future.

Past - Obviously, your company wants to know with whom they are doing business, and whether the person or entity is a channel partner, joint venture partner, or exists under some other business relationship. This is also true for acquisitions. But due diligence is more important than providing a "check-the-box" activity pertaining to the past activities of a third party; it is an important tool in the overall international efforts to fight corruption and bribery. It supports your company's Code of Conduct, protects your reputation, and allows the early discovery of deal-breakers before it's too late. Due diligence will also help provide a legal defense to anti-corruption/anti-bribery laws, like the Foreign Corrupt Practices Act or U.K. Bribery Act. In addition to background and reputation, you need to know third party qualifications before engaging in business.

Present – So what are some types of information that you should obtain in due diligence? The following is a good place to start.

- Identification: It is important to obtain basic identification information on a third party. This includes names, addresses, phone numbers, basic license information, the identities of officers, directors, shareholders, and those who will handle your business and/or be your point of contact. You need to obtain corporate regulatory and partnership filings, a list of countries where the third party does business, and find out if there have been any name changes in the past five years.

- Financial: Your financial review should be based on three years of audited financial records (if any).
- Capabilities: Your review should include a review of the party's facilities, support services, amount of work outsourced, number of employees, and number of years in business. You should also ask for a list of its top 10 customers.
- Government Exposure: You need to determine if the third party does business with any foreign governments or government officials and if there are any government officials otherwise involved with the third party. This extends to relatives and close friends of government officials.
- Enforcement Actions: Here, you need to determine if the party or any of its officials have ever been charged with criminal conduct or been party to criminal proceedings. You also need to make the same inquiries for civil proceedings and/or regulatory actions. It is advisable to review news media stories on the party.
- Internal Control Environment: You should review the party's compliance program, including their Code of Conduct. You should also test their employees' familiarity with the FCPA and/or Bribery Act. See if the company has a written policy regarding gifts, travel and entertainment, and if the employees are trained on pertinent elements of compliance.

Future - The future involves proactive diligence, enabling you to identify red flags in the diligence process before you engage in business with an unwanted party. Diligence, along-side strong contracting and third party training, will become an indispensable tool in your overall enterprise risk management efforts. It is considered a best practice to share your Code of Conduct with third parties and draw attention to internal reporting hotlines for questions and concerns. Key considerations include:

- Clearly communicating that bribery and corruption are not tolerated;
- Using your due diligence to review and improve existing contracts; and,
- Suggesting that the third party adopt a compliance program similar to yours. Alternatively, you may provide training on specific issues.

It is important to note that the "future tense" also speaks to the need for _ongoing_ due diligence monitoring, a critical element and best practice for every program. This is simply because things change. A key partner could be formally charged with a crime two days after closing a contract and only weeks after having performed your "static diligence." The absence of ongoing monitoring will result in little insight into this information. The "future" should really be an indication of perpetuity as well as providence.

Practically speaking, diligence can be performed many ways. In our careers, we have made use of materials and services provided by:

- Transparency International
- Google (and other basic internet search tools)
- World Compliance (www.worldcompliance.com)
- World-Check (www.world-check.com)
- Dow Jones Factiva (www.dowjones.com/factiva/)
- U.S. OFAC databases (https://ofac.data-list-search.com/Search/Simple)

It is important to note that best-in-class vetting systems fully integrate into modern-day ERP systems. Prior to the execution of any transaction, the system performs a real-time background check on selected parties for diligence issues with respect to FCPA, U.K. Bribery Act, ITAR, and much more.

Validation and Oversight

In the compliance world, process validation comes through oversight. More than one of the compliance program standards in the FSG call for companies to monitor, audit, and respond quickly to allegations of misconduct. These highlighted activities are key components for which enforcement officials will look when determining whether companies maintain adequate oversight of their compliance programs.

Many companies fall short when it comes to effective monitoring. Oftentimes, this can be attributed to a general confusion regarding the differences between monitoring and auditing.

- *Monitoring* is **management's** commitment to reviewing and detecting transaction errors in real-time and then reacting quickly to remediate them. A primary goal of monitoring is to identify and address gaps in your program on a regular and consistent basis.
- *Auditing* is an **independent**, targeted, and in-depth review of specific business processes, systems, or transactions. You should not assume that because your company conducts independent audits that it is effectively monitoring. In fact, per the Institute of Internal Auditors (or the IIA), it is Internal Audit's responsibility *to evaluate the effectiveness of management's own risk management functions* (i.e., monitoring). That

audit function should report independently to the Audit Committee of the Board of Directors with a direct line to the CEO or CFO.

A robust compliance program should include separate functions for auditing and monitoring. While unique in protocol, the two functions are related and can operate effectively in tandem. Monitoring activities can occasionally lead to audits. For instance, if management identified a trend of suspicious payments in recent monitoring reports from Indonesia, it may be time to call Internal Audit, under legal privilege, to perform an evaluation of transaction compliance.

Far too often, management looks to the Legal, Internal Audit, or Compliance Department (if standalone from Legal) when something has gone wrong and says, "How could you let that happen? I thought you designed our program to keep us compliant!"

What management is really indicating is that they alone failed to monitor for process and transaction-level errors and use that information to improve their own environment. Conceptually, widgets produced and units sold are of equal importance to the business as actively _managing_ its own people, processes, and systems – the key word being "manage," which is sometimes taken for granted.

Your management team should establish a monitoring system to identify issues and address them. Effective monitoring means applying a consistent set of protocols, checks, and controls tailored to your company's risks to detect and remediate compliance problems on an ongoing basis. Your compliance team can help, for example, by routinely checking with local finance departments in your foreign offices to see if they've noticed recent accounting irregularities. Regional directors should be required to keep tabs on potentially improper activity in the countries they manage. Additionally, a Business Ethics and Compliance Committee should meet or communicate as often as every month to discuss issues as they arise. These ongoing efforts demonstrate your company is serious about integrating compliance and ethics into your business.

The concept of management executing, controlling, and monitoring is also inherent in tangential laws such as Sarbanes-Oxley (SOX). Responsibilities of the certifying officers under SOX are not too dissimilar from the FSG standards. Both require a defined program of internal controls that have established owners and are independently tested for proper design and performance. In fact, many of the internal controls subject to a SOX evaluation would be included in an FCPA program evaluation. For example, think of the "key control" that resides within the Accounts Payable department to evaluate the appropriateness of disbursements in accordance with an established approval authority matrix.

While the two laws have separate objectives, the definition of the control and the nature of the test may be very similar. This is one of the reasons why the SEC plays a key role in FCPA investigations – it is to evaluate the internal controls over financial reporting and ability to prevent or detect fraud. The modern concept of "GRC" (Governance, Risk, and Compliance) would suggest that all such controls be maintained in a central database and tested as one rather than duplicating efforts.

How you audit or monitor can vary considerably. "Old-school" methods of checklist-based auditing have some level of effectiveness, but cannot touch the power of modern, real-time dashboards. In our experience, we've designed data scripts that reside over the top of ERP systems and highlight significant red flags. They provide early warning systems over volumes of data that would simply be impractical for a human auditor to detect. Real-time dashboards might include:

- High discount levels in a particular country;
- Excessive entertainment receipts for a given employee;
- Significant margins on lower margin products; or,
- Higher commission rates or volumes, amongst others.

Finally, as was re-emphasized with 2012's Pfizer Deferred Prosecution Agreement (DPA), your company should establish protocols for internal investigations and disciplinary action. Pfizer's "Enhanced Compliance Obligations" included the following on investigative protocols:

- On-site visits by an FCPA review team, comprised of qualified personnel from the Compliance, Audit, and Legal functions who have received FCPA and anti-corruption training;
- A review of a representative sample, appropriately adjusted for the risks of the market, of contracts with, and payments to, individual foreign government officials or health care providers, as well as other high-risk transactions in the market;
- The creation of action plans resulting from issues identified during the proactive reviews. These action plans will be shared with appropriate senior management and should contain mandatory remedial steps designed to enhance anti-corruption compliance, repair process weaknesses, and deter violations; and,
- A review of the books and records of a sample of distributors which, in the view of the FCPA proactive review team, may present corruption risk.

Prior to such an investigation, however, the company should have procedures – including document preservation protocols, data privacy policies, and communication systems designed to manage and deliver information efficiently – in place to make sure every investigation is thorough and authentic.

A Compliance Department holds some degree of responsibility for marketing the company's programs, both internally and externally (i.e., to in-house employees and applicable, out-of-house third party agents). This "compliance marketing function" educates both employees and third party agents on company and legal standards, processes for reacting to red flags, and methods for reporting violations. Successful "compliance marketing" consists of three key components:

1. Identify: Let your employees and third parties know what you stand for;
2. Incentives: Celebrate employee efforts; and,
3. Tools: Give your employees the tools to participate.

Each of these concepts can play a key role in marketing your compliance program. Let's review them in more detail.

Identify - Let Your Employees and Third Parties Know What You Stand For

In the recently published FCPA Guidance, the DOJ and SEC suggest that the basis of every anti-corruption/anti-bribery program is the Code of Conduct, as it is *"often the foundation upon which an effective compliance program is built. As DOJ has repeatedly noted in its charging documents, the most effective codes are clear, concise, and accessible to all employees and to those conducting business on the company's behalf."*

Two primary goals of any Code are:

1. To document and clarify minimum expectations of acceptable behavior; and,
2. To encourage individuals to speak up when they have questions or witness misconduct.

Incentives - Celebrate Their Efforts

Once again, the recent FCPA Guidance speaks to employee's incentives as of equal importance to disciplinary actions. Does your organization reward for ethical actions?

The Guidance states, *"DOJ and SEC recognize that positive incentives can also drive compliant behavior. These incentives can take many Guiding Principles of Enforcement forms such as personnel evaluations and promotions, rewards for improving and developing a company's compliance program, and rewards for ethics and compliance leadership. Some organizations have made adherence to compliance a significant metric for management's bonuses, much like quality and safety, so that compliance becomes an integral part of management's everyday concern."* It is important to *"...make integrity, ethics and compliance part of the promotion, compensation and evaluation processes as well."*

This concept means going beyond incentivizing. To us, the word "celebration" implies a kind of public display of success. Financial rewards may be given in private, such as a portion of an employee's discretionary bonus credited to doing business ethically and in compliance with the FCPA. Employees who are promoted for doing business ethically are very visible and can act as effective public displays of an operative compliance program. However, we think that a company can take this concept even further through a celebration to help create, foster, and acknowledge the culture of compliance for its day-to-day operations.

Bobby Butler, Chief Compliance Officer (CCO) at Universal Weather and Aviation, Inc., has spoken about how his company celebrated compliance through an event labeled "Compliance Week." He said that he and his team attended this event and used it as a springboard to internally publicize their compliance program. Their efforts included three separate elements:

1. They hosted inter-company events to highlight and celebrate the company's compliance program;
2. They provided employees with a brochure that highlighted the company's compliance philosophy; and,
3. They circulated a booklet which provided information on the company's compliance hotline and Compliance Department personnel.

Tools - Give Them Tools to Participate

Obviously, a key component of any effective compliance program is an internal reporting mechanism.

The FCPA Guidance states: *"An effective compliance program should include a mechanism for an organization's employees and others to report suspected or actual misconduct or violations of the company's policies on a confidential basis and without fear of retaliation."*

The FCPA Guidance goes on to discuss the use of an ombudsman, or a watchdog of sorts, to address employee concerns about compliance and ethics. We do not think that many companies have fully explored the use of an ombudsman, but it is certainly one way to help employees with their compliance concerns.

Interestingly, an interview in the Wall Street Journal, with Sean McKessy, Chief of the SEC's Office of the Whistleblower, McKessy stated that, *"What I hear is that companies are generally investing more in internal compliance as a result of our whistleblower program so that if they have an employee who sees something, they'll feel incentivized to report it internally and not necessarily come to us."*

Identity, Incentives, and Information are three useful tools that companies can use to effectively market their anti-bribery and anti-corruption program efforts.

You have arrived! You have created your compliance program in accordance with FSG §8b2.1, so you're good to go, right? Now all you need to do is sit back and conduct your overseas business with confidence… right? Well, not quite. First, let's first discuss some high-risk areas that deserve additional attention.

As with all other aspects of your business, you are dealing with human beings. When dealing with human nature, the one thing you know for sure is that the potential for disaster always exists. People make mistakes. This chapter provides a partial list of those higher risk areas to actively manage.

<u>Travel, Entertainment & Gifts</u>

Let's assume that your company does not want to fund a multi-year, multi-million dollar bribery scheme violating both its own Code and the FCPA. That's reasonable, right? In this case, how do you best protect your firm when issuing funds for commissions, traveling, entertainment, and gifts? Can you demonstrate an internal control structure that provides real-time visibility into red flags in the expense process? Or, are you counting solely on the detective skills of your Accounts Payable department? Let's take a look by examining some fundamental legislation, statements, and ideas.

A. FCPA Guidance

The DOJ/SEC FCPA Guidance clearly specifies that the FCPA does not ban gifts and entertainment. Indeed the FCPA Guidance specifies the following:

> *"A small gift or token of esteem or gratitude is often an appropriate way for business people to display respect for each other. Some hallmarks of appropriate gift-giving are when the gift is given openly and transparently, properly recorded in the giver's books and records, provided only to reflect esteem or gratitude, and permitted under local law. Items of nominal value, such as cab fare, reasonable meals and entertainment expenses, or company promotional items, are unlikely to improperly influence an official, and, as a result, are not, without more, items that have resulted in enforcement action by DOJ or SEC."*

B. Opinion Releases

Prior to the FCPA Guidance, in 2007, the DOJ issued two FCPA Opinion Releases which offered guidance to companies considering whether, and if so how, to incur travel and lodging expenses for government officials. Both Opinion Releases laid out the specific representations made to the DOJ, which led to the

Department approving the travel to the U.S. by the foreign governmental officials. These facts provided strong guidance to any company which seeks to bring governmental officials to the U.S. for a legitimate business purpose. In Opinion Release 07-01, a company desired to cover the domestic expenses for a trip to the U.S. for a six-person delegation of an Asian government for an educational and promotional tour of a U.S. facility. In the Release, the representations made to the DOJ were as follows:

- A legal opinion from an established U.S. law firm, with offices in the foreign country, stating that the payment of expenses by the U.S. company for the travel of the foreign governmental representatives did not violate the laws of the country involved;
- The U.S. Company did not select the foreign governmental officials who would come to the U.S. for the training program;
- The delegates who came to the U.S. did not have direct authority over the decisions relating to the U.S. company's products or services;
- The U.S. Company would not pay the expenses of anyone other than the selected officials;
- The officials would not receive any entertainment, other than room and board, from the U.S. Company; and,
- All expenses incurred by the U.S. company would be accurately reflected in said company's books and records.

The response from the DOJ states: "*Based upon all of the facts and circumstances, as represented by the requestor, the Department does not presently intend to take any enforcement action with respect to the proposal described in this request. This is because, based on the requestor's representations, consistent with the FCPA's promotional expenses affirmative defense, the expenses contemplated are reasonable under the circumstances and directly relate to "the promotion, demonstration, or explanation of [the requestor's] products or services.*"

In Opinion Release 07-02, a company desired to pay the expenses for a trip within the U.S. for six junior-to-mid-level foreign officials for educational purposes at their U.S. headquarters. This educational trip was to be conducted prior to, but in tandem with, the foreign official's attendance at a six-week internship on foreign insurance, sponsored by the National Association of Insurance Commissioners (NAIC). In the Release, the following representations were made to the DOJ:

- The U.S. company would not pay the travel expenses or fees for participation in the NAIC program;

- The U.S. company had no "non-routine" business in front of the foreign governmental agency;
- The routine business it did have with the foreign governmental agency was guided by administrative rules with identified standards;
- The U.S. company would not select the delegates for the training program;
- The U.S. company would only host the delegates and not their families;
- The U.S. company would pay all costs incurred directly to the U.S. service providers and only a modest daily minimum to the foreign governmental officials based upon a properly presented receipt;
- Any souvenirs presented would be of modest value, with the U.S. company's logo;
- There would be one four-hour sightseeing trip in the city where the U.S. company was located; and,
- The total expenses of the trip were reasonable for such a trip and the training which would be provided at the home offices of the U.S. company.

As with Opinion Release 07-01, the DOJ ended this Opinion Release by stating, *"Based upon all of the facts and circumstances, as represented by the Requestor, the Department does not presently intend to take any enforcement action with respect to the planned educational program and proposed payments described in this request. This is because, based on the Requestor's representations, consistent with the FCPA's promotional expenses affirmative defense, the expenses contemplated are reasonable under the circumstances and directly relate to "the promotion, demonstration, or explanation of [the Requestor's] products or services." 15 U.S.C. § 78dd-2(c)(2)(A)."*

C. Travel and Lodging for Governmental Officials

What can one glean from these 2007 Opinion Releases? Well, it would seem that a U.S. company can bring foreign officials into the U.S. for legitimate business purposes. The Releases also indicate that the following tenants of a Compliance Program should be present:

- Policies and procedures should be established for the company's travel and lodging standards;

- Any reimbursement for airfare should be for economy class;
- The particular officials who will travel cannot be selected (that decision should be made solely by the foreign government);

- Only the designated officials may be hosted, not their spouses or family members (unless the latter are paid for by the foreign government or the families themselves);
- All costs must be paid for directly to the service providers – in the event that an expense requires reimbursement, you may do so, up to a modest daily minimum (e.g., $35), upon presentation of a written receipt;
- Any souvenirs you provide to the visiting officials should reflect the business and/or its logo and should be of nominal value (e.g., shirts or tote bags);
- Apart from the expenses identified above, the foreign government and/or officials must not be compensated for their visit. You may not fund, organize, or host any other entertainment, side trips, or leisure activities for the officials, or provide the officials with any stipend or spending money; and,
- The training costs and expenses will be only those necessary and reasonable to educate the visiting officials about the operation of your company.

Incorporation of these concepts into a Compliance Program is a good first step towards preventing any FCPA violations from arising; however, it must be emphasized that they are only a first step. These guidelines must be coupled with the active training of all personnel. This training must span not only your compliance policy, but also on the corporate and individual consequences that may arise if the FCPA is violated with respect to gifts and entertainment. Lastly, it is imperative that all such gifts and entertainment are properly recorded, as required by the books and records component of the FCPA.

The FCPA Guidance provides examples of improper travel and entertainment; some examples include:

- A $12,000 birthday trip for a government decision-maker from Mexico, including visits to wineries and dinners;
- A $10,000 budget spent on dinners, drinks, and entertainment for a government official;
- A trip to Italy for eight Iraqi government officials, consisting primarily of sightseeing and including $1,000 in "pocket money" for each official; and,
- A trip to Paris for a government official and his wife, consisting primarily of touring activities via a chauffeur-driven vehicle.

Gifts, travel, and entertainment continue to bedevil companies in FCPA compliance. However, in many ways, they are the most straight-forward and process driven components of any compliance regime. If you can put the appropriate standards in place and monitor them in real-time with visual dashboards (via your ERP system), your risk of non-compliance in this area will be substantially reduced.

Distribution Risk

As noted in Chapter 3, a common method of product movement includes the use of distributors. Distributors are common to commercial and consumer products. Distributors differ from other types of sales "representatives" as they take title to products and assume risk of loss. If there was ever a question that distributors were covered under the FCPA, the DOJ has made it clear that this class of entities could be treated the same as any other sales agent (e.g., representatives), reseller, or any other entity which sells a U.S. company's products outside the United States. While the terms "agent," "reseller," and "distributor" have distinct definitions in the legal world, they no longer have such distinctness for FCPA purposes. The question is, "How do you fit distributors into your compliance program while still giving the business distinctions unique to their relationship with your company?"

Let's start with a risk assessment. What do you know about the entity? How long have you done business with them? What is the nature of their financial backing, market, and customer base? Do they work with third parties? Are they representing you to pull sales through the channel and eventually to international sources?

The goal should be to determine which distributors are the most likely to qualify as agents, for whom the company would likely be held responsible. This represents a continuum of risk. On the low-risk end, you have domestic distributors that are essentially domestic resellers with little actual affiliation with the supplier company. On the high-risk-end, you have domestic or international distributors who are very closely tied to the supplier company. These distributors effectively represent the company in the market and end up looking more like a subsidiary than a customer. They may or may not sell to both domestic and international buyers.

Some of risk factors to consider include:

- The volume of sales made to the distributor and the nature of markets served (e.g., domestic vs. international);
- Whether an agreement exists that explicitly prohibits the distributor from markets to whom the company would not otherwise sell (creating an opportunity to circumvent established company policy);

- The percentage of the distributor's total business sales that the principal's product represents;
- Whether the distributor represents the principal in the market, including whether it can (and does) use the company trademarks and logos in its business; and,
- Whether the principal company is involved in the running of the distributor's business through activities like training the distributor's sales agents, imposing performance goals and objectives, or providing reimbursement for sales activity.

Once a company identifies its high-risk distributors, FCPA compliance procedures can be tailored and shared appropriately. For those distributors that qualify as "agents" and also pose FCPA risk, full FCPA due diligence, certifications, training, and contract language are imperative. For those that do not, more limited compliance measures that reflect the risk-adjusted liability are perfectly appropriate.

Management of the Distributor Relationship

Once you evaluate your distributor and ink a contract, your real work begins. You have to *manage* that relationship *going forward*. As do all things in business, price, cost, discounts/commissions, and margins need to be determined. A legal contract may or may not set these parameters. Regardless, organizations should consider the formal means by which they determine how pricing and discounts are offered to a distributor. For this, business organizations might consider the use of a formal Discount Authorization Request (DAR) form.

To do this, a DAR template should be prepared, which is designed to capture the particulars of a given request and allow for an informed, independent, and objective decision about whether it should be granted. Because the specifics of a particular DAR are critical to evaluating its legitimacy, it is expected that the employee submitting the DAR will provide details about how the request originated as well as an explanation justifying the elevated discount. In addition, the DAR template should be designed to identify gaps in compliance that may otherwise go undetected.

The next step is the creation of channels to evaluate DARs. The precise structure of that system will depend upon several factors. Ideally, the goal should be to allow for tiered levels of approval. Three levels of approval are sufficient, but these can be expanded or contracted as necessary. A general rule of thumb to observe is that the greater the potential discount, the more scrutiny the DAR should receive. The goal is to ensure that all DARs are vetted in an appropriately thorough fashion without negatively impacting the company's ability to function efficiently.

The last step is collecting and organizing your evidence of decision-making. Remember, to document, document, document. Once the information-gathering, review, and approval processes are formulated, there should be a system set in place to track, record, and evaluate information relating to DARs. This includes DARs both approved and denied. The documentation of the total number of DARs allows companies to more accurately determine where and why discounts are increasing, whether the standard discount range should be raised or lowered, and provides companies the ability to gauge the level of commitment to FCPA compliance within business operations. This information, in turn, leaves companies better equipped to respond to government inquiries down the road.

This approach has merit because it follows what is set out in the 2013 DOJ/SEC FCPA Guidance, which we will quote from the introductory section of the "Ten Hallmarks of an Effective Compliance Program":

"Compliance programs that employ a 'check-the-box' approach may be inefficient and, more importantly, ineffective. Because each compliance program should be tailored to an organization's specific needs, risks, and challenges, the information provided below should not be considered a substitute for a company's own assessment of the corporate compliance program most appropriate for that particular business organization. In the end, if designed carefully, implemented earnestly, and enforced fairly, a company's compliance program—no matter how large or small the organization—will allow the company generally to prevent violations, detect those that do occur, and remediate them promptly and appropriately."

Email, Email, and Hopefully Less…..Email

From the standpoint of your company's litigation exposure, not much can be more dangerous than its own email history. Why is that so? Well, email is not like contracts, you might say.

First, email is forever. You can't shred email. Even deleting email really just rids a local computer of it; email is backed up and stored on multiple, redundant servers and is nearly always 100% recoverable for an investigation. One of the first things that the regulators will look at is email, as they'll want to understand the discussions that were had, what was committed to and so forth. Whether we're talking about FCPA or any other source of potential legal risk, email has become a very dangerous mechanism in the corporate world.

Second, emails are primarily formatted in a casual manner. It's more like a phone conversation in content—quick snapshots of arrangements to be followed up by a contract or sales order. In many ways, it's the assumed casual nature of email exchanges that can make them extremely dangerous in their relation to the FCPA. As we discussed earlier, the FCPA concerns itself not only with the act of bribery, but also the <u>intent to commit bribery</u>. For example, if a member of your sales team were to write an email to a foreign official regarding a competitive request for a bid and say, "I'll make it worth your while if you put us at the top of the heap," this is incriminating. Even if the deal was never done, it's still as bad as if there had been an actual bribe. The intent to bribe is permanently documented in that email.

Now, think about the thousands, perhaps hundreds of thousands of emails that are sent every day to and from your company. Now imagine the casual language and slang that are undoubtedly used to some degree in their contents. Think about the marketing-oriented language of discounts, sales, and free goods. The words that we use in email are generally not "contract language," and they can become very dangerous when taken out of context. So what's the take away here? There are several that relate directly to email:

- Invest the time to have solid controls around the proper and professional use of email in your organization;
- Educate your workforce about this proper use and reinforce it with ongoing training; and,
- Determine (on advice of counsel and other knowledgeable parties) what an appropriate retention program is and only keep emails archived for the shortest time allowable.

The bottom line is that email can be one of the most dangerous pitfalls you and/or your company face from a legal perspective. Pay close attention to how you use it and control its use in your organization.

Bartering

Bartering is a type of pitfall that isn't necessarily akin to bribery, but could definitely bring your company down the proverbial "slippery slope." Let's say that you're in a oil and gas business and you need something done in a market—a one-time event that might lead to an ongoing arrangement or contract. The third-party agent you're working with wants to be paid in product, not cash. Good deal, right? He will get greater value in product than he would in cash, and you'll save money! Well, wait a minute. Red flags should be flying high right now. How do you substantiate such a transaction? There is no formal contract that spells out the terms of the deal or establishes the value of the products or services. The potential for trouble abounds in circumstances of bartering.

Free or Promotional Product

If you've ever been to an industry convention, you've probably seen plenty of free, promotional material given out. But wait, couldn't this be seen as a bribe? Well, let's take a few steps back first.

There are several types of free or promotional products that need to be considered. First, are the promotional "trinkets" that are given out by sales forces everywhere—free hats, pens, coffee mugs…things of that nature. Most of the time, gifts given in this manner are too insubstantial to really exert much influence an individual. But, as with most things, this depends on the nature, extent, and context of the "promotional" gift. Handing out hats with your company logo isn't a big deal. But if you were to fully outfit an entire foreign police department with product from your consumer clothing business, well that's a different story. Free and promotional products, when used properly, are a tried-and-true means of marketing your business and product. Unfortunately, it's also a very slippery slope with blurred lines. We suggest you always err on the side of caution when disseminating free gifts, even when for entirely benign, legal purposes.

The next type of free product is the "evaluation sample." This is when you disseminate trial versions of your product as a means of demonstrating its merit. For instance, let's say you have submitted a competitive proposal on a bid with multiple companies competing. You decide that because you believe the experience of your product is superior, you want to send a sample of the product to the potential client. In order for it to not be considered an "intent to influence" violation, it must be clear that the product is a review sample and it must be returned to the company. You are then responsible for following up and making sure that the trialed product is returned.

The third type of free product is the "buy ten and get five free" type of promotion. In reality, it's not much different than just lowering the unit price and that cash difference could, in some cases, be considered a bribe. Again, in situations like this, nature, extent, and context are everything. Companies run promotional campaigns like this all the time to boost sales and increase brand-awareness. Why? Well, because it works! However, if you're offering a "buy one get twenty free" campaign exclusively to a particular, high-interest individual, don't expect that excuse to fly.

Discounts and Sales Commissions

Sales commissions can be a very risky area, especially when you are dealing with contract or third-party agents in foreign markets. Let's say you have a third-party sales agent operating for you in Russia. Your goal is to ultimately sell your product or service to the Russian government. Given the culture of Russia, your third-party requests a little something to "sweeten the deal." If you wanted to commit bribery (and conceal it) to effectively lock in that particular sale, you might artificially inflate the sales commission to that third-party sales agent. In this manner, the marginal increase in sales commission would act as an effective bribe. This might also happen without your knowledge, as it very well may be the way business is done in that particular culture. What might be acceptable as commission in one country might not be in another. The important thing is to set a commission structure, document it, and stick to it.

Discounts can be another very risky area that requires careful documentation and a consistent policy. For example, if you are selling directly to a government entity and give that entity an inordinate discount, it operates in the same manner as a bribe. It's no different than giving that customer cash.

Split Transactions

Split transactions can be a real can of worms. The legality of split transactions is fundamentally quite complicated. Let's look at an example. Let's say you have a sales agent in Canada. He executes a sales contract for you and instructs you to send 50% of the commission to him and the other 50% to his brother in a different location. If you don't know what role his brother played in the transaction (or if he played any role at all), then you're going to have a harder time convincing a government investigator of the transaction's legitimacy. From an investigator's perspective, those commission dollars look suspiciously like a bribe. Ultimately, you can legally use split transactions. However, you have to be able to substantiate and verify the reason behind it. When engaging in split transactions, understand that the burden of proof irrevocably rests upon your shoulders in the event of an investigation.

Tax Evasion

The same caution that applies to split transactions can apply to tax evasion. It's possible that an overseas third-party sales agent would want to have all or part of their commission sent to another location in order to circumvent their own country's tax laws. This isn't necessarily bribery, but it will certainly raise the eyebrows of an investigator. It also serves as another example of the necessity of a constant awareness and supervision of those who are working for you overseas.

Third Parties Making Decisions for You

In an effort to wrap up the pitfalls section, we're going to step back real quick and finish the section with some broader, more encompassing concepts.

The most important takeaway from all of this is that, as a leader of your organization, you should be cautious when allowing third parties—whether they be your sales agents or government officials—make decisions for you in a foreign market. For the most part, those sales agents and/or foreign officials will not be held accountable for whatever actions they take on your behalf; you and your company most certainly will. Two things that you must remember are:

- You need to make sure that all monies, discounts, or gifts that are given are relevant to the nature of the transaction, the environment, and the work that's being performed for you; and,
- You must substantiate exactly where the money is going. You must document it with a contract. If, for example, a foreign government says it needs free product because it's part of their quality testing procedures, that needs to be an explicit part of the contract.

Because of the globalization of business, organizations—and not just the big ones—are becoming increasingly distributed. This is in part, no doubt, to an increase in outsourcing. Regardless, and as a function of this, businesses are becoming increasingly decentralized. It's far easier for a CEO to set the rules for one group of ten buyers in one location than it is for him to set the rules for five groups of two buyers in five different locations. This is especially so when you consider his or her obligations to monitor their activities. Organizations that attempt to operate in multiple countries with multiple transaction and/or decision-making points are at heightened risk. Consequently, organizations like this are in greater need of the protection of a robust compliance and monitoring program.

Internal control concepts aren't always given the utmost degree of respect or priority, despite the fact that they are designed primarily to protect corporate officers, shareholders, and general stakeholders.

We've actually heard clients say, "Our counsel provided FCPA training, so I think we're okay. Accounting takes care of our internal controls." Statements like this are red flags, as they demonstrate an unsophisticated attitude towards compliance. This general lack of expertise can manifest itself in intensely dangerous ways.

We assume that you are now familiar with the core tenants of FSG §8b2.1 and recognize that training is but one *small* element in a program. In addition, remember that that even training and internal controls together don't constitute a full-fledged compliance program.

Think about it in the following contextual driving example. Let's say you're new to driving. You've never driven by yourself before, but you've been provided automobile operator training. You now think you know what you're doing, but you're still a little unsure. Well, regardless of what you do, there are still a number of technological and mechanical features that serve as controls to limit error. For instance, let's say you're on the highway and you accidentally bump into the gearshift. Game over, right? Well, no. The car company was provident enough to design the system against accidents like that. In order to shift the car from Drive, the car has to be still and the driver's foot must be on the brake. This is an example of an internal control. The car company trusts its drivers, but only so far. In order to maximize the safety of their vehicle, and minimize the risk of driving it, the company designed a myriad of failsafe mechanisms to prevent a single incident from causing disaster. Internal controls work the exact same way for your company. A well designed and optimized set of controls not only increases transactions activity but makes it safer.

Training your personnel on FCPA, U.K. Bribery Act, and/or broader anti-corruption/anti-bribery responsibilities is a fantastic start. But it's only a start. How does your Accounts Payable Department know that a sales commission to be paid to an international agent actually matches the original contract signed by your executive team? Because your sales team said, "OK to pay?"

Without proper internal controls, your business could suffer from a lack of guidance and direction. While you can train your employees to operate efficiently and ethically, you still have to set controls in place to ensure that these ideals of ethics, efficiency, accuracy, and compliance are continually put into practice. Internal controls will allow you to place trust in not only your employees, but also in a number of failsafe systems set in place within your operations. This way, if a single "system" fails, another will take its place. Let's review some quick points about effective internal controls.

Effective internal controls:

- Are essential to the long term success of not only a compliance program, but your business as a whole;
- Relieve some of the stress associated with the ongoing management of both employees and third parties;
- Provide greater confidence that financial and managerial reports required by DOJ and SEC are accurate;
- Provide reasonable boundaries in which employees and third parties can operate; and,
- Add to the overall health and success of a company.

Truth be told, internal controls are occasionally viewed as a set of burdensome rules and procedures (or added bureaucracy), which are designed to constrain how a person conducts business. This couldn't be further from the truth. In reality, internal controls are essential building blocks of your Enterprise Risk Management structure.

Internal controls promote a culture of honesty, so that individuals do not cheat or steal from the company. Internal controls helps drive data integrity so that reporting tells an accurate story about the transactions being executed. They will also not only increase your ability to monitor the processes of your business, but, in doing so, increase your employees' and hired third-parties' understanding that they are responsible for their actions.

Every FCPA enforcement action on record (that we could find) indicated some lack of internal controls, the extent to which directly impacted fines, penalties, settlements, and time served. Had proper internal controls been set in place, the severity of these consequences would likely have been lessened, and in many cases could have been avoided altogether.

While most compliance practitioners will certainly be familiar with internal controls as mechanisms of detection, the best internal controls help to *prevent* compliance violations before they happen. Internal controls are a "structure of checks and balances" that can:

1. Compensate for human ethical weakness; and,

2. Provide necessary support to individuals of integrity who are facing unethical behavior.

More specifically, internal controls provide assistance to compliance regimes. In other words, they are designed to not only prevent cheating but promote doing business ethically. They'll also aid you in the swift detection of any compliance violations that are occurring behind closed doors.

Internal controls work by helping to set the expectations of the ethical behavior which are required of a company's employees. They do so in a couple of ways. First, they narrow the scope for unethical behavior. They do this in tandem with an increase in the risk of discovery and punishment. Having internal controls in place also acts to train employees in proper practice and procedures. In their constant guidance by management-implemented control systems, employees will begin to act compliantly reflexively. Internal controls can also help protect employees who report unethical behavior. This final point is not to be discounted when considering the Dodd-Frank and Sarbanes-Oxley Whistleblower protections and the Dodd-Frank whistleblower bounty.

Lastly, internal controls aren't necessarily about rules and regulations as much as they're about a company's *operating* culture. A commitment to internal controls is a commitment to doing business the right way. You'll find that by establishing and celebrating a culture of ethical business, these values will become instinctual and self-fulfilling. By making compliance an eminent foundation of your business, employees will adopt compliant attitudes in the workplace; these attitudes will further feed the culture of your business. Internal controls are a vital aspect of this process.

The most effective controls are those embedded "in the line" of a transaction. This means that they are being used directly by line management and not simply the company's finance or accounting group. In this manner, such internal controls have become the responsibility of management and not simply a corporate function, like Internal Audit.

Furthermore, when management is allowed to believe that Internal Audit "owns" its internal controls (which they do not), an "us against them" mentality can develop. Internal controls are management's tools, not Internal Audit's. It is management's responsibility to design, implement, and execute internal controls with Internal Audit's guidance as needed.

Audit's primary responsibility is *to assess the design and effectiveness of those controls* in the company's pursuit to follow the original four areas as provided in the Framework of the Committee of Sponsoring Organizations (COSO) of the

Treadway Commission. That is, internal controls should be designed to assist the organizations ability to:

- Execute strategic plans;
- Operate efficiently and effectively;
- Produce accurate financial and managerial reports; and,
- Maintain compliance with policies, procedures, and applicable laws.

What executive wouldn't be in favor of something that helps achieve his or her personal, financial, and professional process goals?

As with a "safety first" doctrine, successful management teams have determined that the activities elevated with internal controls are critical to efficient and effective operations. With everyone working under predetermined and prescribed principles of guidance, a sense of unity and camaraderie will quickly develop between strategy teams, departments, and co-workers. Simultaneously, a company implementing effective internal controls will tremendously mitigate its risk and liability. Some of the positive contributions that internal controls provide include:

- Limitation of asset loss from employee or third party theft;
- Limitation of single point failures in management behavior by requiring segregated duties and cross-functional review;
- Preservation of accurate information allowing management to better run its business; and,
- Limitation of claims, judgments, lawsuits, and monetary damages.

Think, just for a minute, that the cost of an FCPA violation could be millions of dollars. The financial stakes of potential lawsuits or theft could be even higher. How much less would you have spent on effective internal control assessment and design to begin with?

Simply put, internal controls are the governors that increase your likelihood of a successful outcome, not much different than the feature in your car that prevents a sudden, unwanted change from Drive to Reverse. They're your safety net, the automatic antivirus-software that continuously monitors your PC. With robust and efficient internal controls set in place, the efficient operation and financial buoyancy of your operations no longer exclusively hinge upon the vigilance of your employees.

Okay, okay. So internal controls are good—you get it. Now you want to know a little bit about how to implement them, right? Well, consider the following internal controls as tools to reduce higher risk areas of your anti-corruption/anti-bribery program.

<u>Third Parties</u>

- Always conduct due diligence of third parties prior to engaging in a relationship. Due diligence should be independently spot-checked as part of a recurring audit program.
- Make sure to verify all third-party business entities, including their physical domicile and in-country business bank account(s).
- Ensure that written obligations exist describing a requirement to comply with the Company Code of Conduct, anti-bribery/anti-corruption laws. In addition, make sure to execute any necessary training of employees.

<u>Gifts/Hospitality, Travel and Lodging</u>

- Conduct pre-approval of the amounts offered to third parties to ensure they aren't offered questionable gifts in the midst of competitive procurement.
- Make sure that invoices/receipts are itemized and approved prior to reimbursement.
- Establish written obligations for compliance with local law and define that no items be offered to influence decisions.

<u>International Disbursements/Commissions</u>

- Establish a process of pre-approval and matching for disbursements related to commissions or marketing expenditures prior to disbursement. Matching should consist of ties to an original contract, verifiable receipts, and internal approvals to issue funds.
- Strictly prohibit payments in cash or to private accounts.

<u>Pricing, Discounts, and Commissions</u>

- Establish worldwide pricing and commission thresholds. Deviations from such standards or the offering of free product should be approved by a cross-functional group. Any modifications must be re-routed for signature.

<u>Order Fulfillment</u>

- Establish system-related internal controls that prevent the fulfillment of an international order prior to clearance under the due diligence process.

These are all examples of strong internal controls. By fundamentally aiding their ability to manage and lead, internal controls not only directly aid the company, but its employees as well. Internal controls aren't just about protecting Corporate's best interests. Internal controls are helpful for all members of an organization. Sure, they help manage a company's risk, but when you consider the fact that internal controls also aid middle and lower-tier employees by guiding them in their day-to-day efforts, a sounder picture begins to develop. Simply put, there is no exclusivity on the benefits reaped by well-maintained internal controls; internal controls help everyone do their job better. That's why they're so important.

<u>Knock. Knock.</u>

You get a call one day and a representative of the Federal Government tells you that you and/or your company is being investigated for alleged bribery under the Foreign Corrupt Practices Act. Don't panic! Here's what happens and some guiding thoughts.

<u>Determine Who Is Investigating You</u>

The DOJ is the government agency that has ultimate jurisdiction in FCPA cases. However, there are typically several other agencies involved. Sometimes, investigations are handled exclusively by the DOJ. However, extensive cases, or those that involved undercover work, may require the oversight of the Federal Bureau of Investigations (FBI). In addition, it is likely that the SEC would follow up to investigate any books and records violations. In other countries, an investigation could be subject to the local government and its laws. For example, an investigation under the U.K. Bribery Act might be led by the UK Serious Fraud Office (SFO). Regardless, your first step is to establish exactly who is investigating you.

<u>Hire Counsel</u>

Hiring an attorney is a critical step in the investigative process. This is to ensure you are properly represented and that matters related to the investigation remain privileged and confidential. Ideally, you should hire a firm that is experienced in e-Discovery and anti-bribery/anti-corruption investigations. You also want said firm to have considerable experience in both forensic evaluation and matters pertaining to the SEC.

So, while your first reaction might be to call your existing corporate counsel, such reaction might be a mistake. You need a firm that has depth and breadth to cover the wide range of aforementioned areas. Independent counsel can be hired by the executive team, your General Counsel, or the Board of Directors. This decision is highly dependent on who is being investigated and what the investigation is about. In most public company investigations, it is advisable for a party furthest from the management action to retain counsel (e.g., the CEO and/or the Board).

It is likely that the DOJ may not have the extent of resources needed to conduct a thorough and extensive investigation on their own. To guide the process along, you should consider your use of independent council and the earnestness of your cooperation. Full cooperation with the DOJ and the retention of independent counsel that can perform an investigation on the DOJ's behalf is often met with positive response. However, just because counsel was retained by the organization, that does not permit the concealment of potentially pertinent information. Transparency and full disclosure, where applicable, is a given and should be handled appropriately by your counsel.

Isolate Your Possible Issue

If you suspect (even without full evidence) that a violation exists, it is important to isolate the cause of the potential violation. Any action the company takes in response should be carefully considered in the context of the investigation. However, if one of your employees was charged, you may chose to put that individual on administrative leave. If a severe situation develops, it is advised to stop all deals with selected third parties and/or sales to a particular government.

If you chose to continue your business endeavors during the investigation, methods should be established to ensure transactions are compliant then and in the future. Obviously, any transactions made will be under heightened scrutiny during a Federal investigation. During the course of the investigation, and for a period thereafter, it may be a good idea to elevate your internal controls beyond normal, practical operating standards. Think of your business like a sports team. Typically, during practice, you want to ensure you're playing by the rules. But when it's game-time, the rules carry an additional importance. When the officials are watching and the cameras are rolling, you're going to want to make sure that the rules are a top priority.

Obtain an Independent Assessment of your Program

Alright, so you know who's investigating you, you've hired counsel, and you've identified the potential sources of the violation. Now, it's time to assess where you stand. Your counsel will likely hire a creditable audit firm that can be used to independently evaluate your organization's transactions and internal controls. These reports should be provided directly to counsel and be maintained under privilege. More importantly, this will likely become the foundation of your future remediation project plan.

An independent evaluation could be quite exhaustive and consist of aggregating multiple years of transaction activity. To whom did the company make sales pitches? To whom did it sell product? Who contacted the company? What were the details of all deals made? Which third parties were active in each engagement? What discounts were given? Who authorized them? Yes, it's a long list. But the information gained from each and every one of these questions is indispensable. You need to catalog everything: the flow of funds, as well as all paper and electronic communication. This is the backdrop and environment from which you want the investigation to proceed. The investigation can go in multiple directions, but the two most likely courses that the DOJ will take are to: (1) follow the money; (2) follow the communications.

Because, at its base, the FCPA and U.K. Bribery Act are about bribery, following the money is critical. Your investigation could look at deals consummated, deals not consummated, and all of the details therein. They might not just look at the flow of the money, but how approvals were documented and how the transactions were recorded. This could starts with the request for bid, the initial quote given, the pricing offered versus what was paid, what was offered in addition to pricing, and whether or not a formal contact was established.

They may also look at all the communications related to establishing the deal. This may come down to individual emails. Were there any planned or unexpected trips back and forth during the course of the deal? Were any gifts given? Travel and entertainment reports could be examined to see if money or gifts were used for inappropriate purposes. After a deal was consummated, was the company paid in a timely fashion? Where did the funds originate? When were the commissions paid? What type of documentation suggests the payment of commissions? Were the commissions sent to the business address or a home address? Were they split? Remember, these are all questions that have to be answered for a single deal. You can see how arduous and time-consuming a process this becomes from the perspective of the company under investigation.

Part of the investigation may include an examination of archived email history. This could include a number of searches related to terms related to the particular deal. For instance, popular searches might be for the country name, the salesperson's name, the name of the product, and keywords like "discount" or "bribe." As evidence is slowly pieced together, a cohesive picture could slowly develop.

Expectations for Length and Outcome of the Investigation

DOJ investigations are laborious. Often, the official investigation will continue for several years after all of the actual investigative activity has been concluded and all results have been shared. Even though they have nothing more to ask, the DOJ has limited resources and will take its time as needed. They are going to tend to gravitate toward the largest or most probable cases, so their resources could shift around. Expect an investigation to be protracted and painful. In all likelihood, the requests from investigators won't cease until the investigation's end.

A number of potential outcomes could come from the investigation. One is that nothing happens (cross your fingers for this one). The others span the gamut of potential legal ramification. In some cases, fines will be charged to the employees and officers responsible—these are fines for which the organization may not pay. Fines may also be levied against the organization itself. In situations, implicated parties may be imprisoned. In the very severest of circumstances, the government may appoint a "monitor" who is assigned to oversee all activities at your company for a specific time, usually between two and four years.

Paul McNulty—former Deputy Attorney General—often cites three questions he would ask a company under investigation by the DOJ:

1. What did you do to prevent it?
2. What did you do to detect it?
3. What did you do after you found out about it?

The FCPA Guidance phrases these three points of emphasis slightly differently, encouraging the tripartite of *prevention, detection, and remediation* in the framework of your anti-corruption compliance program. The cost associated with a failure to receive a "passing grade" on any of these questions can be astronomical. This past year, two more companies entered the list Top Ten of all-time FCPA settlements: Total S.A, ranking in with $398 million in fines, and Weatherford International with $152.2 million. That's a lot of money.

The largesse of these fines mirrors a growing, global and popular sentiment against bribery and corruption. In other words, while the considerable size of these fines demonstrates extensive FCPA violations, it also demonstrates direct and extensive efforts to fight bribery and corruption on a Federal level. The size of these fines not only sends a message to the corporations to whom they are levied, but also to all other would-be violators: the United States does not take bribery and corruption lightly.

What's more, this general trend extends far beyond the boundaries of the United States. For example, consider our past references to the Chinese enforcement action against the British company GlaxoSmithKline in 2013. Here, Chinese authorities introduced and enforced their own country's domestic anti-corruption laws, not a foreign-focused law such as the FCPA. This demonstrates a genuine and uncontrived eagerness to battle corruption in the global market. No longer does the United States stand out as one of few nations who staunchly stand against bribery and corruption. Anti-corruption is now a global initiative.

The individual perspective of anti-corruption and due process is of an equal importance. After all, a good deal of bribery and corruption occurs on an individual, not corporate, level. However, even the most honest individuals may become involved in something not-so-honest, either out of ignorance or just plain bad luck, and the policies in many countries do not favor innocent bystanders. For many western ex-pats who are considering working in internationally, this may cause them to rethink whether or not they are willing be stationed in the country for fear of being caught up in another country's judicial system, which is a system not known for protecting individual due process rights. This factor cannot be overstated – because being imprisoned in a place like China is near the top of just about anyone's list of things you never want to experience.

Remember at the beginning of this book when we asked you to take out a piece of paper and a pen and document your answers to selected questions? Now, let's do that again.   This time, we're going to provide the answers that we've presented you throughout this book. Before you look to see what we've written, try it out on your own. By comparing the answers you've written by memory and those we've provided below, you'll be able to identify any areas that you might want to revisit.

How does your organization limit the risk of non-compliance? Can you list the controls?

We limit the risk of non-compliance with a multi-faceted program that includes a balanced set of internal controls. These include:

- A program that meets or exceeds the expectations set forth in the Federal Sentencing Guidelines' "Effective Compliance and Ethics program";
- Detailed company policies and substantial in-person and on-line training delivered through a corporate university;
- In-depth vetting of third parties and high risk transactions;
- Independent, cross-functional review of high risk disbursements; and,
- A Business and Ethics Council and an appointed leader of compliance.

Do you know what the prevailing standard and U.S. Government's expectations are for a compliance program?

Yes, those standards include, paraphrased:

- Leadership and Tone from The Top
- A Commitment to Compliance – Beyond the Tone
- Measurement: Set at Zero Tolerance; There is No Materiality Standard for Corruption and Bribery
- Standards and Procedures
- Education and Training
- Efforts to Exclude Prohibited Personnel – Due Diligence
- Validation and Oversight

Can you point to (or touch) your compliance program? What about your Ethics Program?

Yes. It is documented in our anti-corruption/anti-bribery program. This can be found on our corporate intranet and it is delivered via in-person training to our staff on an annual basis. Our Ethics Program is maintained by our Ethics Counsel and led by our CEO. She has a copy of the Code of Conduct and supporting activities of the organization.

How do you mitigate the risk of bribery?

We mitigate the risk of bribery through a series of policies, preventive and detective internal controls, and an employee training program. These are monitored independently on a periodic basis by our Internal Audit department. Some of these policies include:

- We introduce and enforce prohibited activities policy which prohibits bribery facilitation payments or free goods to foreign officials;
- We require a cross-functional review of discounts and commissions outside of established, written standards;
- We require a multi-point matching process in Accounts Payable that compares contracts to executive approvals to requests for payment;
- We strictly coach and audit business operations involving travel, gifts, entertainment, and gratuities; and,
- We do not allow single point approvals anywhere in the control environment.

When was your last independent anti-corruption/anti-bribery program audit?

- We've scheduled one for next quarter.

Made in the USA
Charleston, SC
10 August 2014